IMAGES
of America

CHICAGO
HEIGHTS

IMAGES
of America

CHICAGO HEIGHTS

Dominic Candeloro and Barbara Paul

ARCADIA
PUBLISHING

Published by Arcadia Publishing
Charleston, South Carolina

Library of Congress Catalog Card Number: 00-102540

For all general information contact Arcadia Publishing at:
Telephone 843-853-2070
Fax 843-853-0044
E-mail sales@arcadiapublishing.com
For customer service and orders:
Toll-Free 1-888-313-2665

Visit us on the Internet at www.arcadiapublishing.com

Cover Photograph: Chicago Heights was in its golden age in the 1940s and 1950s. Energetic young second-generation ethnics went off to war, won, and came home in the late 40s and 50s to enjoy the peace and prosperity they had created. In this 1942 photo, inductees and their friends gather before boarding buses bound for military training camps. In the background are the icon structures of the heart of their city, Chicago Heights.

CONTENTS

About This Book

This photo book is a first step toward creating a comprehensive history of Chicago Heights. The authors and the members of the Historical Preservation Advisory Committee culled through more than a thousand images in the library archives to choose photos representative of the city's history. We also made an appeal to the public to share their photos with us for our project. And while there are many limitations to this process of documenting history—unidentified photos, uneven distribution of photos with regard to time periods and topics—the resulting book is a splendid chronicle of the people and places of Chicago Heights. This affordable volume puts a priceless collection of photos within the reach of every home and school in the city.

It will answer many questions about our past and (we hope) make our fellow citizens curious to learn more about the colorful history of our town. We invite your feedback. If you have more information about the photos in this book, or if you seek more information about them and what they depict, we urge you to consult the Chicago Heights Free Public Library. A draft of this publication along with additional identification for some group pictures will be on file in the library. There, you will also find our complete photo archive, much of which was collected by Louise Michalek and the old Chicago Heights Historical Society. The microfilm files of the *Star* from 1906 to the 1960s are rich with detailed coverage of all types of activities in the city. The library also has an extensive indexed collection of Declaration of Intent and Citizenship papers, the manuscript census (1900, 1910, and 1920), and an alphabetical obituary file as aids to family historians.

We also invite interested readers to donate or lend for copying additional photos, films, and videos relevant to the history of Chicago Heights. These will enrich the archive and provide material for future exhibit or publication projects. The Chicago Heights Historic Preservation Advisory Committee believes that the understanding and preservation of our past is essential for our community's future. Appreciation for the past engenders the sense of pride and self-confidence that we, as individuals and as a community, need for successful development. The toil, struggle, and success of the pioneers, immigrants, and industrial and commercial leaders of Chicago Heights should encourage in all of us a "can-do" spirit. If they could create a great city, so can we. Since history is an ongoing dialogue, we invite all local history buffs to join with our Chicago Heights Historic Preservation Advisory Committee at 7 p.m. in the library the second Tuesday of each month.

We owe a debt of gratitude to dozens and dozens of friends, and we do not wish to slight anyone. However, we would be remiss if we did not thank Louise Michalek, the late Nick Zaranti, Mayor Angelo Ciambrone, and all the members of the Chicago Heights Historic Preservation Advisory Committee: Elizabeth Booth, Barbara Demith, Genevieve Ford, Joseph Hawkins, Earlene Levesque, Ester Montalvo, Marie Patton, Dolly Pinnow, Jeanne Rafaj, and Karen Siegrist. Also, thanks to Geri Biamonte, Carol Candeloro, Mary Orlick, Paulnita Rees, Claudia Ruiz, Steve Modzelewski, and our tireless photographer, John Spomar. Special thanks to all of the donors at the photo fair: Jay Allord, Delores Arcadia, August Barberi, Irene Baker, Joan Bauer, Jennifer Buttell, Tassie Cladis, Nathalene Cornish, Camille Damiani, Sandra Draper, Frank Enright, Lawrence Fazzini, Lottie Fik, Marlene Glavas, Bernadine Gwiazda, Williard Heusmann, Fred Jendrasek, George Kline, Minnie Lauteri, Jim Leader, Fred Lobue, Victoria Mancini, Ector Mascitti, Louis Mascitti, Kitty Molyneaux, Jerry Murawski, Charles Nardoni, Emmett Parker, Antoinette Ruesch, Louis Venditti, Janice Ward, Sonja Washington, Thornal Washington, Joyce Weckwert, John Wozny, Joe Yambor, Joe Zarlengo, and Maria Zerante.

Barbara Paul and Dominic Candeloro—March 1998

An Outline History of Chicago Heights

White settlers began coming to our area in the 1830s, during a time when the settlement was known as Thorn Grove. The population increased with the influx of German 48'ers, and in the 1850s the area became known as Bloom. By the 1890s, several railroads served the area and a group of real estate promoters calling themselves the Chicago Heights Land Association purchased a large tract of land to attract industrial development.

At the request of the Land Association, Bloom's name was changed to Chicago Heights sometime during 1892. The head of the association was Charles H. Wacker, a prominent Chicago businessman and chairman of the Chicago Plan Commission. He was so well known at the time that Wacker Drive was named after him.

Both the police department and the volunteer fire department were organized in 1892 in preparation for the expected industrial boom.

In 1893, special C & EI Railroad trains brought prospective investors from Chicago to Chicago Heights. The Land Association promoted Chicago Heights as a manufacturing and industrial center by offering free factory sites, water, and switching facilities, and cheap fuel to companies that located here.

The promotion succeeded, and by 1897, Chicago Heights boasted about 20 factories, a bank, 5 schools, nearly 10 miles of water mains, 2 freight depots, 3 passenger stations, and an electric light plant, as well as the Victoria Hotel. There were also 38 railroads serving Chicago Heights, giving the area the best shipping facilities in America.

The promoters were also successful in attracting a steady stream of Polish, Italian, Swedish, Slovak, African-American, and Greek workers to take advantage of the factory and commercial jobs they had created in the new Chicago Heights.

On February 23, 1901, the village became a city. The City Hall, as well as Old Bloom High School, was built during the same year. The city's library was erected as a gift to the people by Andrew Carnegie in 1902.

By 1910, the population of Chicago Heights had reached 14,535. St. James Hospital was dedicated with 50 beds on Thanksgiving Day, 1911. The hospital was the culmination of the efforts of many to provide the growing industrial community with vitally needed medical care.

In 1913, a new post office was erected just south of the intersection of Sixteenth and Halsted Streets. During 1916, the Arché Fountain was built and dedicated to celebrate the intersection of the Lincoln and Dixie Highways in Chicago Heights. The junction of these two great intercontinental highways in Chicago Heights led local boosters to proclaim Chicago Heights as the "Crossroads of the Nation."

The Lincoln-Dixie Theater, with its imposing design and luxuriously tapestried interior with seating for 2,500, opened on June 23, 1921, to serve the 20,000 residents of Chicago Heights.

In 1933, Chicago Heights celebrated its centennial anniversary of settlement with great enthusiasm.

The Bloom High School building located at Tenth Street was opened in 1934 with the help of students who carried desks and books from Old Bloom to the new building. The Art Deco structure was placed on the National Register of Historic Places in 1982.

Many of Chicago Heights's finest young men served in the armed forces during World War II, while those left at home worked many hours of overtime supplying sorely needed war materials.

In the 1950s, Prairie State College was established as Bloom Community College, dedicated to fulfill the educational needs of local residents. Marian Catholic High School began enrolling students in 1955.

By the 1960s, the number of school-aged children had increased dramatically. Kennedy School opened in 1964, and the new Bloom Freshman-Sophomore division on Sauk Trail opened its doors to 1,050 freshman in September 1964.

During January 1967, Chicago Heights, along with other surrounding communities, was battered by the Great Blizzard. Twenty-seven inches of snow fell in 33 hours.

Despite the demise of several industrial employers, the seventies and early eighties proved to be a time of building. The new library building opened to the public on August 5, 1972. The city's new Municipal Building and the Safety and Justice Building were occupied in 1976. As part of the city's contribution to the nation's bicentennial celebration, the Arché Fountain was rebuilt in its original location at the intersection of Lincoln Highway and Chicago Road. In the fall of 1979, the Chicago Heights Park District Recreation Center opened, and Bloom Township Hall became occupied in the fall of 1981.

Today, Chicago Heights has over 30 churches, 50 industries, numerous businesses, and a score of public and parochial schools with over 11,000 students.

One

PIONEERS AND
PROMOTERS

Settlers came to Chicago Heights at about the time that Chicago was incorporated as a city. The German, Scotch-Irish, and Easterners founded the first church in 1843. Growth was steady until the 1890s, when the city became a boomtown. Our photos burst with the energy and optimism of the building boom of that era. In a short 20 years, the city promoters created both an industrial powerhouse and a regional market town.

This is where it all started—today's Thirteenth Street and Chicago Road. In the spring of 1833, Absolem Wells and his family became the first white settlers in southeast Cook County. Located on the ridge south of where the Hubbard Trail crossed Thorn Creek in an oak grove that still remains, Wells's cabin stood in the same spot for 50 years.

From the First National Bank's series by John Keast, this image of the Native Americans in the woods is probably very much like the scene encountered by Absolem Wells. Wells grew attached to the native Pottawatomi, and tradition has it that he married a Native American woman and traveled west with their tribe as they were pushed out of Illinois.

A color mural of this image depicting pioneers on Sauk Trail was also part of the bank series by John Keast, an artist and interior decorator who lived at Euclid and Main (Northwest). His work evokes the life and landscape of the 1840s, the time when Chicago Heights was settled.

By 1901, the original Adam Brown house, which was located at Brown's corner where Hubbard's Trail (Chicago Road) met Sauk Trail, had been enlarged and was known as Burgel's Tavern. The site served as hotel, tavern, stable, and popular place of entertainment (including carnivals and circuses) for local residents for many generations.

James Hunter built this country store c. 1866 on the west side of Chicago Road (Hubbard's Trail, north of the Michigan Central Railroad tracks) after he and Stewart Eakin dissolved their partnership. It was later operated by Vollmer Bros.

Pioneer farmer and banker William James McEldowney stood in the yard of his home located at 149 West Fourteenth Street in the 1880s. The rear portion of the home was moved to this rural spot from a location on the west side of Chicago Road near what is now Nineteenth Street. In the spring of 1880, he added the two-story structure in front of the original one, and it remains there today as Karen and Terry Siegrist's private Victorian home.

A crowd of Sunday excursionists brought out by the Chicago Heights Land Association in the early 1890s came out to see the new development. Hundreds of excursionists stayed on to take jobs in the new factories mushrooming on the east side of the city, and many purchased lots to make their homes in Chicago Heights. The building in the background is the old auditorium.

The band played while the prospective buyers streamed in from the special C & EI train which brought them to the new community that promoters promised would become a busy and prosperous manufacturing center. Charles Wacker and Martin Kilgallen were leaders of the Land Association, which, in the 1890s, used all kinds of stunts to sell the public on their real estate enterprise.

13

The Chicago Heights Land Association offered free transportation and other inducements to the public to visit Chicago Heights for the sales pitch. Seen here on June 12, 1893, this summer Sunday crowd appears to be large and enthusiastic. The slogan was "Chicago Heights: The Men, The Land, The Money."

Led by President Wacker, members of the Chicago Heights Land Association Board of Directors gathered in Chicago Heights in 1892. The city was promoted as a planned industrial community on the 4,000 acres purchased from farmers in the area. Farms which had been purchased for $1.25 an acre in 1840 sold for 100 times that figure in the 1890s. Many factories sprung up almost overnight in the 1890s and 1900s, as the Land Association offered free water, free switching facilities, and free factory sites.

This scene shows rough riders on Chicago Road c. 1890.

Workers laid the cornerstone for the new City Hall at Sixteenth and Halsted Street in 1901. The building housed the city and police offices, as well as a basement jail, until it was destroyed by fire in 1953 with the loss of one life. Mayor John W. Thomas is pictured standing with his back next to the derrick leg.

Two

EARLY BUSINESSES

The resourcefulness and the courage of early business people in Chicago Heights was phenomenal. How they got together the capital, the energy, the genius, and the will for success in small business is impressive to the modern reader. Confidence in the future, family solidarity, and the prodigious immigrant work ethic were key elements here. One is also struck by the boosterism and pride of Chicago Heights civic leaders—a pride that lasted well into the 1950s.

Keast had an idyllic view of the prosperity created by heavy industry and railroads in Chicago Heights. This was the perfect image for display in the bank building from the 1920s to the 1960s.

This rural image also came from the Keast bank series. Until the 1960s, Chicago Heights was a market town for the surrounding rural area. Farmers in South Holland, Beecher, Monee, and Matteson looked to Chicago Heights for their banking, transportation, entertainment, and shopping needs.

An unidentified conductor with motorman Herman Mantz (on the right) pose with the "Dinky," a train that transported people within Chicago Heights and linked up with interurbans making connections with towns like Joliet and Kankakee. Public transit between these towns was better then than it is now. In addition, advertisements were as important to businesses at that time as they are today.

Mr J.W.Thomas
and Mr. P.D.Block and
group of Steel workers.

Inland Steel and Calumet Steel were booming businesses, offering employment to thousands of skilled and unskilled immigrant workers. At one time, folks boasted that there were so many unskilled jobs in Chicago Heights that workers could, without any notice, quit work at Calumet Steel on one day and start work the next morning at Inland or any of the other big manufacturing plants on the East Side.

This station was on the B & O line which operated along Stewart Avenue on the Hill and East Side until approximately the 1960s. In the 1920s, the building was adapted for use as a field house for old Lincoln Center (now Martin Luther King) Park.

Chicago Terminal Hotel, located at 1401 Center on the East Side near the B & O roundhouse on Stewart Avenue, is pictured here in 1912. The original owner was Julius Oertle. The hotel served railroad crews, new immigrants, and workers at nearby Hamilton Piano and Morden Frog factories.

Teamsters lined up at the railroad station to deliver people and goods to their destinations.

Old Passenger Station of Chicago + Eastern Illinois R.R. and Michigan Central R.R. and Tower at the Crossing

This view is looking north at the old passenger station and tower where the C & EI met the Michigan Central. The Michigan Central came to Chicago Heights in 1853, and ran east and west along what would have been Eighteenth Street. Its route has been used for the Old Plank Road Trail bicycle path.

James Ward, here with his horse in the early part of the century, was a pioneer Black entrepreneur on Fifteenth Street who dug basements for a living.

21

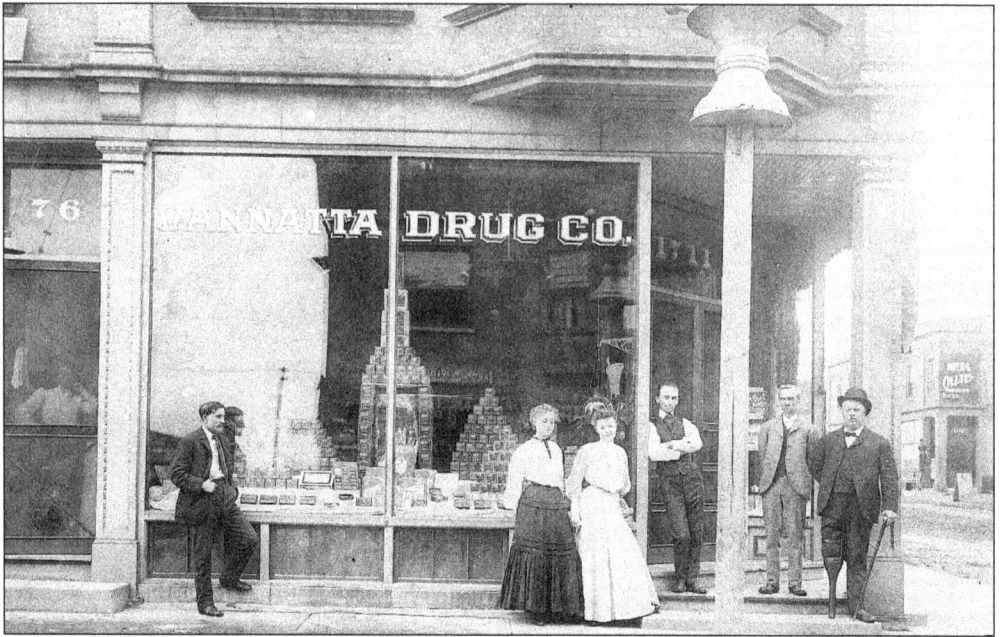

Seen here in 1902, Vannatta's Drug Store was located on the southeast corner of Illinois and Halsted Streets until it was later moved to 6 East Illinois Street. Vanatta served as township highway commissioner from 1916 to 1918, and was an avid supporter of the Lincoln Highway Association. Note the pharmacist's mortar and pestle on the pole in front of the store.

Before the advent of the automobile and supermarkets, the itinerant fruit peddler was a neighborhood regular. Seen here in 1906, Sicilian immigrants Francisco LoBue (left) and Iggie Formati pause along their Otto Boulevard route.

22

Waddington Meat Market was a fixture in downtown Chicago Heights for decades. This 1898 photo illustrates the abundance of fresh meat available to Chicago Heights residents and the pride the individual shopkeepers had in their businesses. Waddington's trademark was a large white plastic pig displayed in the front window.

Thomas W. Booze Barbershop was located at Oak and Illinois Street c. 1902. In this photo, Mr. Booze appears to be welcoming Eagle State Convention participants to avail themselves of his services. Old Illinois Street remained a center for small shops, restaurants, clothing stores, and hardware stores until the 1970s.

23

An early delivery vehicle suggests humble beginnings for the Rau Department store, which was to become the largest and most stylish department store in town, located at Sixteenth and Otto Boulevard.

In the early part of the century, goods and materials arrived at railroad storage depots and were distributed by horse and wagon throughout the city. This is a scene of the Tossetti Brewing Company, located next to the railroad, c. 1905.

LABOR DAY PARADE Serving the Community for 46 Years Chgo. RD. before it

Until the 1950s, coal was the basic fuel for both industry and home heating. Old homes on the Hill and East Side still sport coal bin windows. Independent ("not incorporated") was one of half-dozen coal companies serving Chicago Heights.

Francisco LoBue, the proud owner of the grocery store located at Twelfth and Portland, posed with his family and horse in 1909.

25

Art Richert tended bar in his tavern located at the northeast corner of Main and Halsted in 1919. Note the calendar.

The Hildeman Plumbing
office was located at 23 Illinois
Street near Oak *c.* 1910.

Italian Co-Operative Grocery,
located on East Fourteenth Street,
was opened by local socialists in
1911 with 101 owner/members.
It functioned into the 1930s,
with Umberto Lisciani serving
as manager for many years. The
structure grew to house offices, a
bar, banquet hall, and club rooms.

Dixie Dairy milkmen gathered along Nineteenth Street in 1926. The bow-tied supervisor is Anthony Skirba, and the man wearing the suit is C.B. Eskilson. Horses plied milk routes in Chicago Heights into the 1940s; early-morning home delivery was accompanied with clomping hooves and the clink of milk bottles.

This is Keast's view looking west on Lincoln Highway crossing Thorn Creek in 1921, just a few years after the opening of the first transcontinental highway. Homes in the background are today among the city's most prized residential structures. Farthest right is the home of W.W.M. Davis (built in 1919), the pre-Depression president of the First National Bank. In the foreground is McEldowney Park.

In the 1920s, Pagoria's garage and filling station on the north side of East Fourteenth Street provided taxi and towing service for local customers, as well as gas and repairs for cross-country travelers on Lincoln Highway.

George Kalcic posed with his delivery truck in the 1940s. Home refrigerators and clean natural gas heating units eventually eliminated the need for this delivery service.

These young boys were *Star* newspaper carriers *c*. 1926. The best source of information about the history of Chicago Heights is the microfilm record of the *Chicago Heights Star* from 1906 until the 1960s. Published twice weekly by the Williams family, the *Star* contained detailed information on the political, economic, religious, and social lives of the city.

On Illinois Street in the 1930s, the Kouchis Brothers were part of a small but energetic Greek-American business community in Chicago Heights.

"Number please?" The telephone company in the 1600 block of Otto Boulevard provided good jobs for young ladies. Two digits, four digits, twelve-party, four-party, and two-party lines were common in the early years. The SKyline prefix and seven-number dialing came into fashion in the 1950s.

Each fall saw the introduction of "revolutionary" new models of automobiles. Into the 1950s, Halsted Street, north of downtown, and Chicago Road combined to make "automobile row" for Chicago Heights. In this photo, South Suburban Motors introduced the 1938 Studebaker in their North Halsted Street showroom.

Employees at the First National Bank of Chicago Heights celebrated the business's 25th anniversary with a cake and flowers. Note the dressy nature of business attire in 1954.

Three

CHICAGO HEIGHTS AND WORLD WARS I AND II

As an industrial immigrant city, Chicago Heights played a big role as supplier of men and materials for both World Wars. The chemical companies, steel companies, tool and die companies contributed mightily to the war effort. The age cohorts of the sons of immigrants matched the needs of the military draft in both wars. Our photos don't illuminate the Depression experience in Chicago Heights, but the message of support and commitment to the nation during the wartime crisis comes through loud and clear. The war years and the post-war prosperity were truly the golden age of Chicago Heights.

Attired in coats, ties, and hats, young Chicago Heights residents gathered on the north lawn of the Public Library to answer the WW I draft call on February 22, 1918.

This view shows the post–World War I Armistice Parade. Because Chicago Heights was a growing young community, more than its share of young people were drafted into both World Wars. Heavy industry like chemical and steel factories were also vital to both war efforts.

During WW I, postal employees participated in fund-raising and morale-boosting efforts on the homefront. The dark-suited man in the center is Postmaster W.H. Stolte.

Chicago Heights residents turned out in great numbers to celebrate the end of WW I. This scene is at Halsted and Seventh Street. Note the cobblestone brick streets and the trolley tracks.

This groups of selectees departing for army induction was described by the *Star* as the second African-American contingent to receive a send-off in Chicago Heights in July 1942. Pictured on the front row far right is Rev. F.C. Trotter, pastor of Union Evangelistic Baptist Church.

Chicago Heights inductees pose on the steps of the Carnegie Library before leaving for basic training *c*. 1941. Throughout the war, the *Star* regularly ran photos of white and African-American (segregated) groups bound for war. Identification for many of the men in this photo is available in the Chicago Heights Public Library files.

Draftees assembled here before departing for WW II. Businesses pictured in the background from left to right are as follows: the Victoria Hotel, Cohen's Men Furnishings, Citizen's National Bank, Harry Yaseen Jewelry, Ames Dress Shop, and F.W. Woolworth. Note that this group photo is similar to, but not identical to, the cover photograph.

President Franklin Roosevelt posed with a giant globe donated to him by Earle Opie's Weber Costello Company of Chicago Heights. Exact replicas were also given to Stalin and Churchill so that the leaders would have a common reference globe when planning military strategy. One of the original globes is now on display in the Bloom High School Library.

Lt. Norman E. Albrecht, who lived at 1649 Oak Street, received the Bronze Star from a colonel in Paris in October 1945.

From 1904 to the mid-1980s, Columbia Tool was a sizable manufacturing plant that employed hundreds and played a vital role in the WW I and II efforts. In 1962, it became a prime supplier of the hot work tool dies used in fabricating parts of the Gemini Space Capsule. The plant was located on the southwest corner of Lincoln Highway and State Street.

Mayor Joseph Gannon spoke from Tony Mascitti's front porch on Fifth Avenue in a neighborhood flagpole raising ceremony honoring the mothers and other relatives of men serving in World War II. In both men (from all ethnic groups) and material (from the booming factories), Chicago Heights contributed mightily to the war effort.

Four

Downtown
Chicago Heights

Nostalgia for Chicago Heights's old downtown is universal among our residents aged 50 and above. It was the heart of the city—where the action was. It was a place to see and be seen. It was the backdrop for pageantry and commerce. The old downtown—Halsted and Illinois Street—was not just a banal place where merchants rented stores to sell goods to people, it was the institutional setting for our lives, offering comfort, stability, and a sense of place. It was a commercial district that also offered spiritual and emotional benefits.

A 28099   Illinois Street showing Victoria Hotel, Chicago, Ill.

This postcard view of Illinois Street looking west is from 1910. Note the horse-drawn wagons, clock tower, and commercial signage. Also note the misidentification "Chicago."

This aerial view shows downtown Chicago Heights c. 1950. The Lincoln-Dixie Theater, Victoria Hotel, and the old City Hall form a triangle of the three most prominent buildings.

42

The layout of the downtown area as a walkable commercial district is as clear as the growing need to find adequate parking.

The Victoria Hotel was constructed in 1892 to accommodate overflow visitors to the Columbian Exposition in Chicago. Designed by Louis Sullivan with characteristic arches, it was a good anchor for the new planned industrial suburb. In later years (1940s), the first floor housed a Walgreen's, Del Giudice's Jewelry, Foley Travel Bureau, the Donovan Agency, and various cigar and clothing stores. Ravaged by fire and demolished in 1961, it was the showpiece of Chicago Heights for four generations.

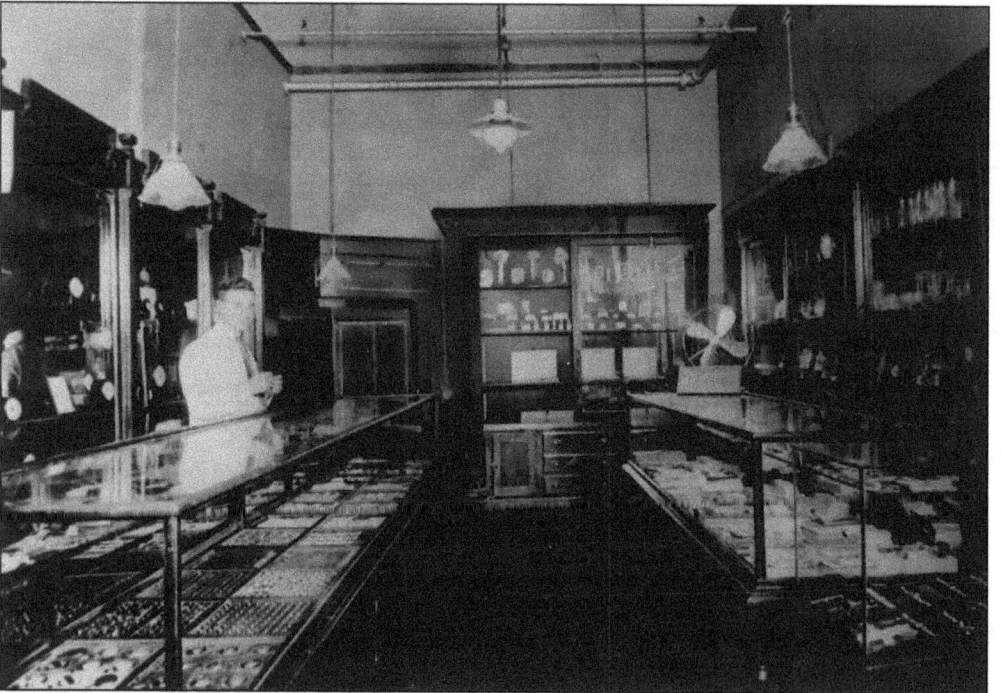

Italian immigrant jeweler Angelo Del Giudice proudly displayed his wares in the shop he maintained in the Victoria Hotel from the early 1920s to the early 1960s. This photo is dated from the 1920s.

In this 1910 photo, businessmen relaxed in the Victoria Hotel's bar in the ambiance of sumptuous wood paneling, cigars, spittoons, and of course, Rover.

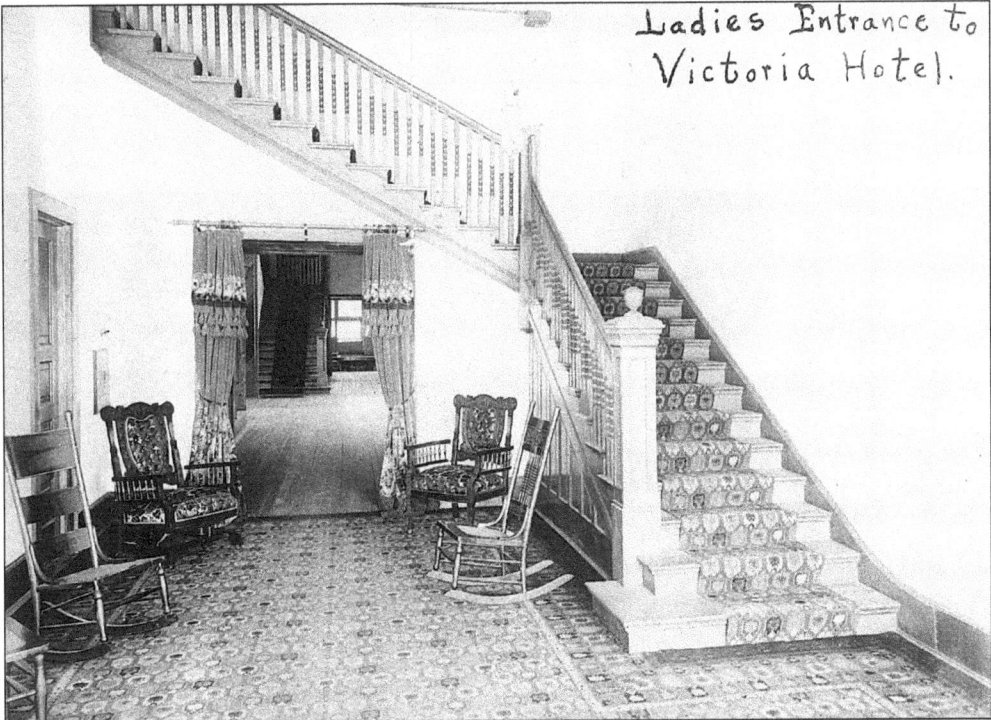

Ladies Entrance to Victoria Hotel.

A separate ladies' entrance to the Victoria Hotel reveals the detailed wood treatments in the hotel, as well as the Victorian manners that segregated the genders in the early twentieth century.

As shown in this photo from August 1930, Kappmeyer's Cigar & Stationery Store was located in the Victoria Hotel.

A dad and his daughter stop at the Arché Fountain at the crossroads for a refreshing drink of Chicago Heights well water in this 1920s photo.

The Free Public Library was financed by Andrew Carnegie in 1902, and was located at the very heart of the downtown shopping district. The popularity of the business district eventually caused parking problems that led retailers to spread out into shopping centers like Park Forest's.

The basement level of the Carnegie Library was reserved for children. Today, many adults remember the old library fondly as the place where they were first introduced to the joys of reading—just as Andrew Carnegie had planned it. This third-grade class from the East Side shows off their book selections.

Seen here *c.* 1930, this temple of prosperity was erected in 1910 by the McEldowney family. Originally the Citizens Bank, it later became known as the First National Bank of Chicago Heights. Its interior featured stained-glass windows and a rotunda with murals illustrating the history of Chicago Heights.

The interior of the First National Bank exuded grandeur, strength, and formality. Both the exterior temple design and the interior design were important to the image of banks, as so many of them failed after the stock market crash of 1929.

In 1913, construction of the Post Office building began on the east side of Halsted south of Sixteenth Street. Note the solid construction, location near the railroad station, and the trolley tracks on Halsted Street. The interior featured dark oak woodwork, a mosaic floor, marble baseboards, and trimming—all built at a cost of $50,000. In a controversial move, the Post Office was relocated to West End Avenue in 1958.

In 1911, St. James Hospital was a comparatively modest structure, established in Chicago Heights as the regional center for medical attention. Staffed by the Sisters of St. Francis, the institution grew and changed with the times, surviving even the decline of the old downtown in the 1960s and 1970s.

Western Union and the telephone company shared this building on Otto Boulevard where they employed about 20 workers in 1913. Note the telegraph messenger's bicycle parked at the light post. Also pictured are the five-light lamp post, Thoeming's grocery store, and a wagon.

The Thomas Hotel, located on the southeast corner of Seventeenth and Halsted, was built by the Thomas family in June 1923. It later became the Albert Hotel.

When it was built, the proud 83-room hotel building rivaled hotels in Chicago for modernity and luxury. Fabled coach Alonzo Stagg attended the Thomas Hotel opening. It was destroyed in this fire in 1979.

In the late 1930s, the Lincoln-Dixie Theater sported a classic marquee and a long vertical sign. To the left of the entrance is the Karmelcorn shop.

The Lincoln-Dixie Theater opened on June 23, 1921, and was demolished in 1972. It had fallen on hard times, and even the venerable Karmelcorn Shop had moved. The sign, however, points the viewer one block north to Chicago Heights Federal Savings and Loan, a new (1950s) colonial brick structure.

This is the proscenium stage of the Lincoln-Dixie Theater c. 1930s. This photo reveals a full orchestra pit, elaborate box seats, organ, stage curtains, and extensive seating. The Lincoln-Dixie was one of a score of fabulous 1920s movie houses built in the Chicago area.

The fabled Lincoln-Dixie Theater, visible looking north on Chicago Road and Illinois Street c. 1941, accommodated 2,500 for vaudeville, operas, and cinematic performances. Schultz Drugs and the Citi Service gas station were other Illinois Street/Chicago Road landmarks.

This winter railroad scene near the C & EI station between Sixteenth and Seventeenth Streets was photographed sometime in the 1940s. Railroad trains have plied their way through town on four main lines—the old Michigan Central (Eighteenth Street), the C & EI (along East End Avenue), the old B & O (Stewart Avenue), and the Chicago Heights Terminal Transfer Railroad, which connected the others and served the factories on the East Side. Residents learned to live with the noise, soot, and traffic snarls, which were the by-products of the railroads.

With the onset of WW II, the early 1940s brought rationing and lines at the Kneip Market on Illinois Street.

In the late 1940s, the east side of Halsted directly north of Seventeenth Street featured Jordans Men's Wear, J.C. Penney, Hartman's Department Store of home furnishings, and the Chicago Heights National Bank. Note the Thomas Hotel sign.

This *c.* 1951 view looking south on Halsted and Otto Boulevard from the old City Hall shows the 25-foot-wide Jewel grocery store on the right, and the late-1940s vintage cars parked at an angle to maximize parking capacity.

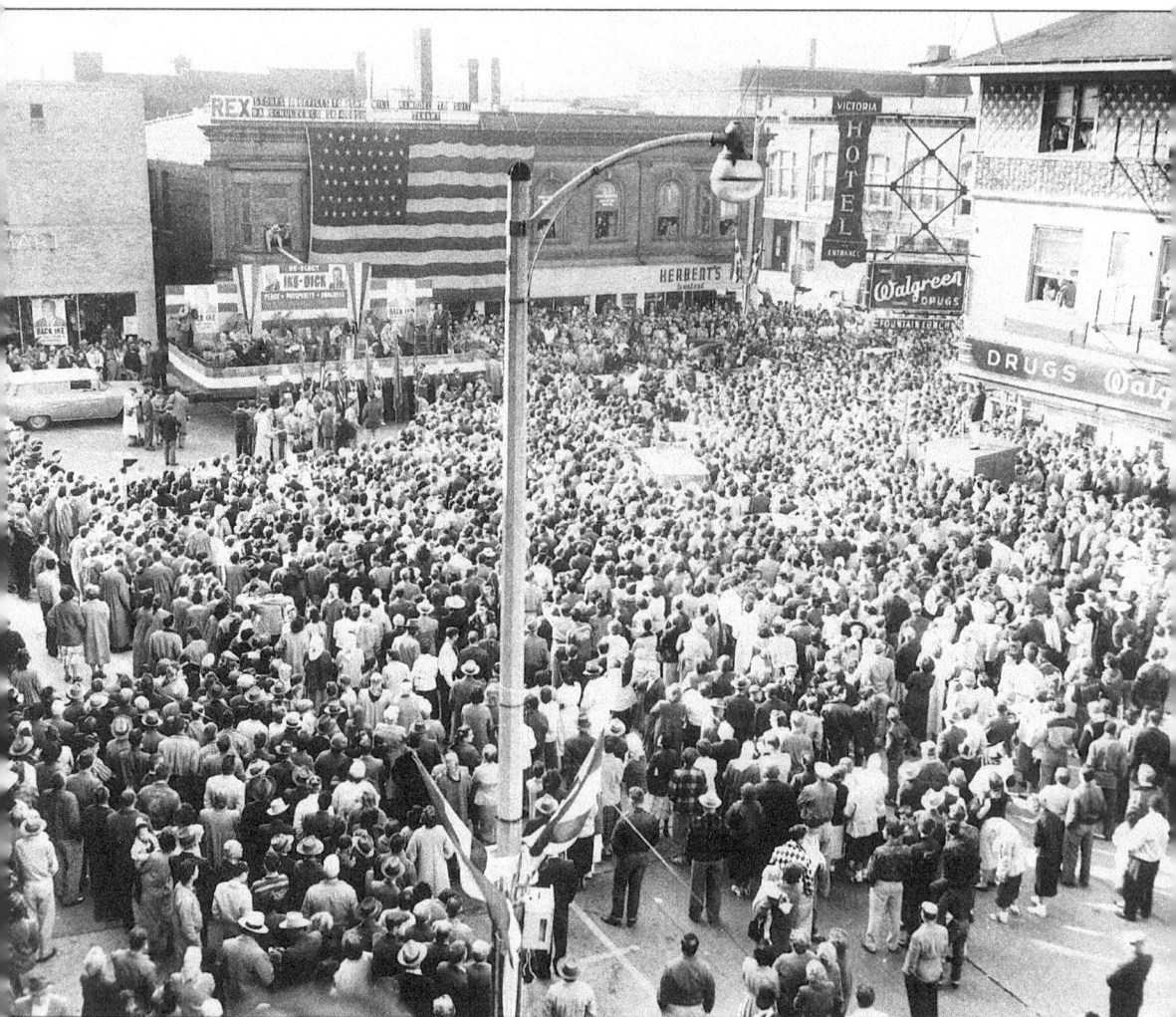

This is a scene from the podium on that special day in 1956 when Richard Nixon and Governor Stratton brought the presidential campaign to downtown Chicago Heights.

The local Republican organization was very successful in getting out a large crowd for Vice President Nixon and Governor Stratton on this fall day in 1956.

As shown in this view of the north side of Illinois Street in the early 1960s, the E-Z Snack Diner visually dominated the middle of the block. Angle parking had long been used to maximize parking spaces in the downtown area.

Looking east on Illinois Street from the roof of the Lincoln-Dixie Theater in the late 1950s revealed a bustling shopping center, water tower, smokestacks, and St. Joseph's steeple (pictured top left). Note also how Illinois Street took a jog at Oak, and how many storefronts had second- and third-floor apartments above them.

The late 1950s saw one of St. James Hospital's major expansions. The St. Paul Lutheran Church is visible to the left.

Looking east on Lincoln Highway from East End Avenue in about 1930 reveals the way that Lincoln Highway traffic contributed to the city's economy. The location of Lincoln Highway was undoubtedly a key to the success of the Pagoria Garage and other auto-related businesses there.

Kline's Department Store, shown here in the 1960s, was famous for its ability to cater to the tastes and fashion preferences of three generations of Chicago Heights residents. Kline's served the Heights in a variety of locations, including this one on the west side of Halsted, north of Sixteenth Street, until it finally closed in 1995.

This site is the location at which Otto Boulevard met Halsted, and where the men of Kiwanis built Santa's house in the 1950s. Apparently, Schiff's Shoes and Thom McAnn were tough competitors that season. Of course, the biggest treat for youngsters in that era was a visit to the second-floor carousel at the Rau's Store.

This photo taken from the second floor of the Rau Store shows a sidewalk sale in the 1960s. Otto Mall had replaced the old City Hall, and Otto Boulevard was closed to traffic. The store pictured at lower left is Walgreen's and at right is J.C. Penney.

63

An aerial view of St. James Hospital, the new library, and old Bloom–City Hall in 1974 emphasized the prevalence of two-story frame residences in central Chicago Heights, while also illustrating the progressive expansion of the hospital.

Five

PARADES

The number of parade pictures in our collection is large both because it was a good opportunity to take pictures, and because parades were frequent and popular among the people of Chicago Heights. Whether it was Good Roads Day, Youth Day, Progress Day, or the Fourth of July, groups and organizations felt a desire and obligation to show their sense of community and to show off and impress the public.

Boiler Makers union members posed for a Labor Day, 1910 photo in front of the standpipe water tower on the south lawn of City Hall. Note the early streetlight.

Apparently this is a night-time celebration of the end of WW I in November 1918. The dense crowd at Seventeenth and Halsted included a cross-section of the population. The photo exudes the residents' strong sense of community.

Teams of horses leveled roads on Good Roads Day. This is also a unique view of the entrance of the original bank building, which stood on the corner of Seventeenth and Halsted until it was replaced by the terra-cotta structure that sits there today.

On Good Roads Day in 1916, teams of horses gathered in front of the bank after smoothing out Lincoln and Dixie Highways. Note the details of signage and street "furniture."

This view of the Youth Week Parade heading up Illinois Street shows the brick pavement on the streets.

A rain-soaked Youth Day Parade in 1929 headed west on Illinois Street turning south onto Chicago Road. Vannatta Drugs, Public Service, Spindler Koelling Funeral Home, and Copitelli Music store signs identify businesses on the south side of Illinois Street. Note also the trolley tracks and mounted police.

This is the Fraternal Order of Eagles parade float in front of the Post Office, seen sometime after 1913.

As part of a parade, young people marched up Illinois Street past the Citi Service Station that sold "gasolene" and advertised its rest rooms.

This photo documents the diverse and interesting architecture of the commercial buildings on the east side of Halsted during the 1937 Progress Parade.

This is another view of the Progress Parade, which took place on October 16, 1937.

This Progress Parade in 1937 was the culmination of a week-long celebration meant to instill confidence in the economy during the Depression era.

A band performed in the Progress Parade and headed south on Halsted. The *Star* reported that 25,000 people watched this parade.

American Legion Post #131 headed south on Halsted *c*. 1940. In the background, Florsheim Shoes and the Rau's Store are pictured.

In 1951, this parade headed south on Halsted.

Crowds gathered on the library steps and along Halsted as the parade headed north during the era when Hartman's Department store and Butler Women's Clothing store operated on the east side of Halsted.

Henri Buttell began his musical career in the Bloom High School Marching Band in the 1930s. The Henry Buttell Orchestra played for generations of proms, weddings, dances, New Year's Eve parties, and various celebrations at local service clubs and dance halls from the 1930s to the 1980s.

This 1962 photo of a parade coming from the east reveals the intensity of commerce on Illinois. The Bonath twins taught tap dancing and ballet to generations of Chicago Heights children.

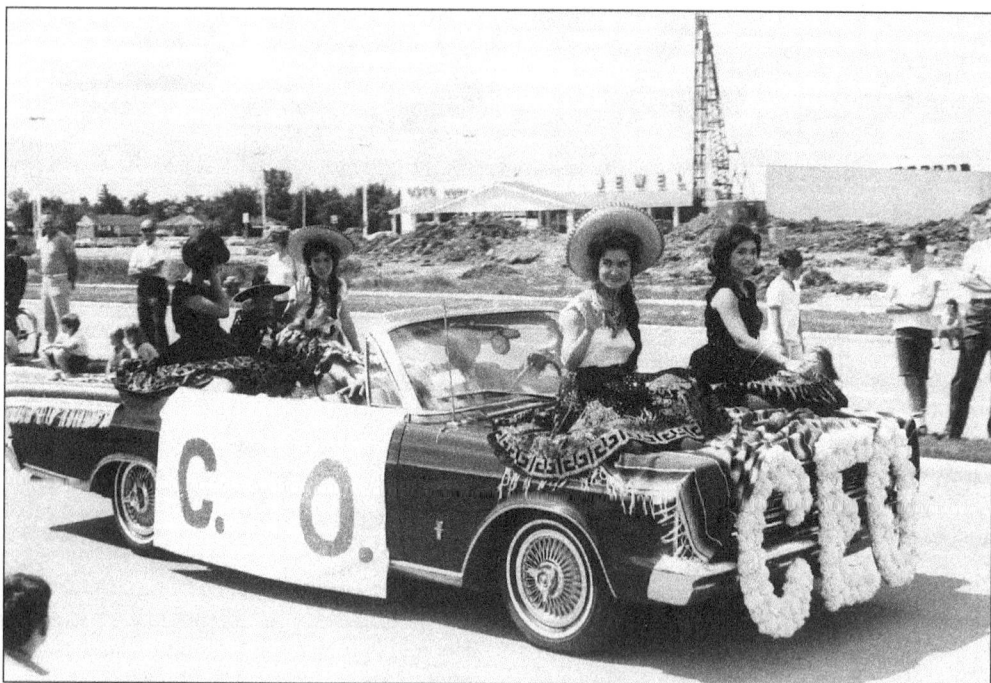

Mexican Americans from the Committee on Economic Opportunity participated in a Fourth of July Parade as it passed Bloom Market in 1967.

Six

CITY SERVICES

This section documents photos connected with the city government and its employees, especially the firemen and the police. Respect and tradition are themes of most of these photos, although "just plain fun" seems to be the theme for the Dan Bergin car photo. A full exploration of Chicago Heights's political history must wait for another publication.

The first mayor and city officials of the city of Chicago Heights appear here after its official incorporation as a city in 1902.

The fire department was organized on April 10, 1892, as a volunteer group. Pictured in the center of this 1895 photograph is Chief Horace Scott, holding his brass speaking trumpet that he used to shout out orders to his men during a fire.

Alderman August Kasdorf celebrated his installation in 1906 with friends at the Hotel Victoria.

This *c.* 1895 photo shows a horse-drawn hose cart.

This photo, taken on Halsted Street *c.* 1900, shows a horse-driven hook and ladder unit.

Until 1895, the fire equipment was *hand* drawn. This photo shows a horse-drawn fire engine *c.* 1905.

The Chicago Heights Fire Department's equipment was on display in front of Station #1 on Nineteenth Street *c.* 1930. The station was completely decked out with a brass pole and a Dalmatian mascot.

Mayor Dan Bergin stood in a car surrounded by a crowd in front of the Lincoln Theater. Apparently, the group was marking the opening of Chicago's 1933 Century of Progress Fair by inviting motorists on their way to the fair to visit Chicago Heights, despite the fact that the newly improved strips of the Lincoln and Dixie Highways had not been officially approved as World Fair routes.

In 1938, motorcycle, foot, and squad car police patrols protected our city. What appears to be the full force posed here in front of the Sixteenth Street entrance of the City Hall–Police Station building.

This 1924 photo of the police department was taken on the south lawn of City Hall looking north. Thoeming's, E.C. Sturm, and the Rau Store building appear in the background.

Chicago Heights's finest posed on the steps of the old Post Office in 1950. The civilian in the center is Commissioner John Gansen.

The police force posed on the west side of City Hall in the 1950s. Mayor Maurino Richton is the civilian on the far right.

Dr. Anna Medaris, pioneer Chicago Heights physician and the first woman elected to a public office in Bloom Township, came to Chicago Heights in 1900 to practice medicine. She was elected Bloom Township supervisor in 1914.

Seven

Neighborhoods

Before the 1960s, the East Side, the Hill, and the West Side were very different than they are today. Bus and trolley transportation, corner stores, neighborhood lodges, clubs, and churches and nearby places of employment were characteristic of the Hill and East Side. The Jones Center played an enormous role in helping newcomers gain new skills and make adjustments to city life. The interaction between ethnic classes and neighborhood groups, while sometimes hostile, made for creative tension—a competition in which the city benefited from its diversity. On the West Side were quiet, stable residences with large lawns reserved for the middle class.

Constructed in 1916, the Harold Colbert Jones Memorial Community Center at Fifteenth Street near Center Avenue delivered social services to generations of Italian, Polish, Lithuanian, and African-American immigrants in the classic social work tradition of Jane Addams and Hull House.

A soapbox derby sponsored by the Jones Center attracted enthusiastic participation from would-be Talamontis (see page 100).

This Jones Center craft project kept young ladies busy as the presence of a camera brought shy giggles in 1941.

The Jones Center provided young and old with a chance to develop skills to succeed in their new culture. This 1930s evocation of the Melting Pot expresses the notion that ethnic groups would melt into the mainstream, even though there was plenty of evidence all over town that the melting process would be slower than idealists had imagined.

During the Depression, the Jones Center provided educational programs and employment in cooperation with the NYA and the WPA. The former included Americanization and English language classes for Italian, Polish, Lithuanian, and Greek immigrants eager to gain citizenship during hard times. Seated above is Albert LaMorticella, who taught English to Italian immigrants and later, Italian to the children of those immigrants.

The first A&P store in Chicago Heights was located at 1444 Fifth Avenue. Throughout the 1930s, the A&P was just another corner store on the East Side. In the 1940s and 1950s, the A&P occupied a larger space on Halsted and Fifteenth Streets.

From the 1890s, the East Side was a multi-ethnic enclave that included African Americans from the beginning. Although the schools and neighborhoods were not segregated, many other aspects of social life were. For more information on African Americans in Chicago Heights, consult the photo exhibit permanently housed in the library.

Seen here in this 1930s view, the Jacob Friedlander Furniture building was located on the southwest corner of Sixteenth and Center on the East Side. Since most residents did not yet own automobiles, neighborhoods provided shopping of all sorts, entertainment, social clubs, and factories.

At Gereg's Grocery Store, located at Twenty-fourth and Butler in 1926, Steve Gereg, Emma Cepek, Edward and Mary Gereg, Mrs. Wloch, Mrs. Beebe, and an unidentified dog (listed from left to right) gather to do business. Corner groceries provided friendly service, convenience, *and* instant credit.

Girls congregated outside the Barrel Ice Cream Parlor, an East Side landmark located at Sixteenth Street and Fifth Avenue.

Every Chicago Heights neighborhood had a shoe repair shop or two. In this photo, Leonard Venditti makes a repair in his father Alex's shop on East Twenty-third Street. Shoe repair shops, barber shops, groceries, and corner bars provided gathering places for residents to exchange greetings, information, and gossip about the community. These shops also provided opportunities for factory workers to put their families to work in creating small businesses.

The Ripani Grocery, located in the 1400 block of Wentworth, was an example of a neighborhood grocery of which there were dozens in Chicago Heights through the 1950s. Eventually, universal access to the automobile and the advent of the supermarket knocked them out of business.

Proud parents, godparents, and family took baby Alfred Tavoletti on a baptism-day spin in what was reputed to be one of the first automobiles in the city, c. 1910.

A landmark watering hole from the 1930s to the present, the 3-Star operated under various managements and was part of the Twenty-second Street commercial area in the Hill section. Besides great beef and sausage "sangwiches," the 3-Star featured fenced-in bocce courts (pictured to the right).

A WW II flag raising at Twenty-first and Butler honored the boys in the service and their families. It was a solemn neighborhood event.

Wakes in private homes were common in Chicago Heights into the 1940s. Here, the Lale family gathers for a final photo with loved one George. The c. 1930 photo was intended to be shared with relatives in Italy unable to participate in the wake and funeral rituals.

In the 1950s, the Chicago Heights Teenage Community Choir, affiliated with the Calvary Missionary Baptist Church, performed throughout the state. One of their most notable performances took place in Park Forest in 1956 when Vice-President Nixon brought his re-election campaign to the area. Adult leaders included Thornal Washington, John Tate, and Clarence McCoy.

"At your service!" Jacob Biamonte manned the cash register at the original Silver Tavern, located at Lincoln Highway and West End in the mid-1920s. During the prohibition era, many venerable bars in Chicago Heights became ice cream shops, candy stores, and luncheonettes.

When Mrs. John W. Thomas, widow of the city's first mayor, left for a round-the-world trip in 1912, her only instructions to architect Irving Kelley was that she wanted him to build her a house with seven bedrooms—the rest was up to him. When she returned in 1913, she found the house shown here awaiting her. In 1939, it was sold to West End Funeral Home.

The Liberty Theater was an East Side institution. Located on the north side of Fourteenth Street west of Wentworth, the movie palace was symbolic of the full range of services available on the Old East Side into the 1950s.

This late-1940s "thrift home" was built by a group of Chicago Heights contractors and subcontractors to satisfy the housing boom after WW II.

This photo of a Slovak Lodge includes many residents from the Twenty-fifth and Butler section of the Hill *c.* 1925. Most residents were also members of St. Paul's Catholic Church. More detailed identification of this photo is on file in the CHPL.

94

This is the Lincoln Highway Bridge over Thorn Creek in winter. Note the lighting fixture and Lincoln Highway emblem on the bridge.

A Sangamon Street block party in 1959 illustrates the post–World War II growth in housing on the north end of the city. Many of the residents had moved to the new sections from over-crowded homes on the Hill and East Side.

A 28072 View of Chicago Heights, Chicago, Ill.

Thorn Creek, the major geographic facet of Chicago Heights, runs southwest to northeast through the center of Chicago Heights in what is now McEldowney Park and Cook County Forest Preserve. Boys with fishing poles and the steel bridge between Fourteenth and Sixteenth Streets are pictured in this 1920s photo.

Hickory St. East of Euclid Avenue, Chicago Heights, Ill.

This 1930s street view shows Hickory Street east of Euclid during road and sewer construction.

Eight

SOCIAL ORGANIZATIONS

The number and variety of social organizations in Chicago Heights before 1960 is impressive and we have the photos to prove it. Service clubs, ethnic organizations, musical groups, dramatic organizations, business associations, and sports teams enriched the social scene in an era before two-income families, color TV, CD music, and air conditioners isolated us in our homes.

This scene shows a turn-of-the-century picnic.

In the late teens and early 1920s, Little Giant trucks lined up east of City Hall to transport workers and their families to a summer picnic. The Chicago Pneumatic Tube Company was the manufacturer of Giant Trucks.

The 1919 Baseball Champs were probably from the Manufacturer's League. As in most American cities, participation in sports was a common means of gaining social acceptance for ethnic males.

The Chicago Heights Concert Band is pictured perhaps on the wooden bandstand in Woodrow Wilson Woods. The drum says, "Inc. 1923." Pictured directly behind the drum is August Nardoni.

The Sauk Trail Chapter of the Daughters of the American Revolution appeared in costume at the home of Mrs. Edna Hawes on October 5, 1929. Complete photo identifications are on file at the CHPL.

Motorcycles were so popular in Chicago Heights in the 1920s that there were a number of "motorcycle funerals." Shown above is one such event down Vincennes Avenue.

A hero of Chicago Heights in the 1920s, Sonny Talamonti was a championship racecar driver in Indiana. He called his car the "Spirit of Chicago Heights," and his followers from our city thronged racecar tracks when he raced. His death in a fiery crash brought great sorrow to many residents.

The 1935 African-American championship baseball team illustrates the segregation of the time period. Baseball on the amateur and semi-professional levels remained of high interest to city residents of all races into the early 1950s, as television brought the Cubs and Sox into our living rooms.

Motorcyclists, equipped with sidecars and brimmed caps, gather at Smitty's garage on the East Side.

Petticoat Fever was performed by the Drama Group in October 1939 at the Washington School Auditorium. Begun in the early 1930s as an offshoot of the Chicago Heights Women's Club, the Drama Group is one of the oldest and most successful community theaters in the nation.

"Pioneers" appear in the Centennial Historical Pageant in 1933. For three nights at the Chicago Heights Athletic Field, residents portrayed their ancestors. The covered wagon and cow were supplied by William F. Heusmann. Numerous Heusmann kin appear in the photo. This image is a reminder that white settlers have been in our area for 165 years—surviving, growing, and prospering.

Active participation in musical groups was more widespread in the early part of the century than it is today. This is the Ashlar Band of Chicago Heights in 1928.

In 1936, the Bloom Township High School Orchestra performed mainly classical pieces. In addition to this orchestra, the city at one time or another supported a large high school band, John Paris's Chicago Heights Symphony, several lodge-based bands, and numerous musical performers in the Drama Group.

Manager Hap Bruno and the Chicago Heights Athletic Association team jubilantly left the field after winning the 1948 Championship.

Into the 1960s, the Kiwanis Club was big enough and energetic enough to field this sizable singing group.

Opened in 1925, the Chicago Heights Park District's Lincoln Center Park wading pool attracted a diverse group of eager young bathers. Construction of the improvement was reportedly sponsored by the Kiwanis Club.

Decked out as pirates, the men of Kiwanis gathered in an empty lot to promote their sponsorship of a circus. The Kiwanis, the Rotary, and the Lions Clubs all played a vital role in cultivating a strong sense of community among the business and professional leaders of the city.

This is the James McEldowney residence *after* it had been taken over by the American Legion at Twenty-first and Chicago Road. From the 1920s to the 1950s, the Legion flourished, at least in part due to the profits from slot machines in the basement.

Eleanor Roosevelt visited Chicago Heights in October 1960 while campaigning for John Kennedy. Posing here with Mrs. Roosevelt are local Democratic leaders including Angelo Ciambrone (second from the right).

Nine

CHURCHES

The town was filled with a wide variety of immigrant groups which tended to focus on their churches for both spiritual and social support. By the 1920s, Chicago Heights had dozens of church buildings, including the impressive First Methodist and First Presbyterian buildings in the downtown area. The spot where the First Presbyterian Church was founded in 1843 is marked by their cemetery at Twenty-first Street and Chicago Road. The church scene has also seen changes in which new groups occupy churches originally built by other denominations and ethnic groups.

The First Presbyterian Church was founded in Chicago Heights in 1843. This building served as their church at Twenty-first and Chicago Road until 1913. The site continues to serve as the Presbyterian cemetery today.

This First Presbyterian Church structure, located at the corner of Sixteenth Place and School Street, was dedicated in 1913 and replaced in 1965 by the current building at Tenth and Thomas. The complete history of this church is available at the library.

The Presbyterian youth group is pictured here in the Euclid Park field house c. 1940. The park district field houses at Euclid and Wacker Parks were built by the WPA in log cabin style. Ashland (Smith) Park and Jirtle Park also have field houses with distinctive designs.

The First Christian Church stood at the corner of Sixteenth Street and Vincennes, near the Rau's Store, c. 1930.

Swedish women and children pose with a minister on the steps of the Immanuel Lutheran Church Parsonage in 1910. A significant share of the skilled metals workers in Chicago Heights in the early years were of Swedish descent.

In the early 1940s, the congregation posed in front of the Italian Presbyterian Church of Our Savior at Twenty-fourth and Wallace. The pastor at this time was Reverend Carducci (mustached, first row right). The church served the cultural and spiritual needs of two generations of Italian Americans in the Hill area.

The First Presbyterian Church had an alliance with the Church of Our Savior (Italian Protestant) and the Jones Center, and sponsored a summer camp to teach English to Italian children. In this c. 1925 photo, Reverend De Luca sat among the students and teachers of this sylvan summer school.

Parishioners streamed out of the Assumption Greek Church at Fifteenth Street and Center following services in the 1920s. The distinctive architecture of the building identifies it as Orthodox. The existence of a Greek church on the East Side illustrates the multi-ethnic nature of the community in those days.

A wedding party and families posed outside Assumption Church c. 1930.

Well into the 1950s, Chicago Heights residents included a small, but influential, Jewish merchant community. The original synagogue was located in the 1300 block of Otto Boulevard. The Temple Anshe Shalom was built on Scott Avenue and Fifteenth Street in the 1950s, and has since become an African-American church.

The congregation of the Payne Chapel posed here in the 1940s. The Payne Chapel (African Methodist Episcopal) is the oldest African-American church in the city. Located on Center Avenue around the corner from the Jones Center, the current church building has a 1923 cornerstone.

112

The St. Ambrose Episcopal Church was erected in 1904 on a site across Chicago Road from St. Agnes Catholic Church. This building was demolished in 1968 when the congregation moved to its current location on MacArthur.

Pictured here in the early part of the century, St. Agnes Church was founded by Irish Catholics. The other Catholic churches in the city were organized along ethnic lines as follows: San Rocco (Italian); St. Joseph (Polish); St. Ann (German); St. Paul (Slovak); and St. Casimir (Lithuanian).

Father Kautakis posed in front of St. Casimir's Catholic Church on the south side of west Fourteenth Street c. 1960. St. Casimir was built by East Side Lithuanians and later, briefly served Mexican Americans.

The groundbreaking ceremony for St. Paul's Catholic Church was held at their new building at Twenty-fifth and Butler.

The earliest members of St. Paul's Evangelical Lutheran Church were Swedish and German immigrants. This structure stood on the south side of Fourteenth Street at the approximate site of the current St. James Hospital Emergency Room until 1956, when the congregation moved to Tenth and Ashland.

Reverend Trotter (pictured left) hosted a state congress of Baptist Sunday School officials at the Union Evangelistic Baptist Church in Chicago Heights c. 1950.

These people were members of the congregation of the original St. James CME Church located at 307 East Sixteenth Street c. 1940. This church now occupies the old St. Ann's (German) Catholic Church at Chicago Road and Main Street.

San Rocco Catholic Church was located at the top of a hill at Twenty-second and Portland. This 1947 First Communion Day photo shows the numerous saints, communion rail, votive candles, and an altar facing away from the congregation, illustrating the essence of the pre-Vatican II decor of the church.

The funeral photo in front of San Rocco in the late 1920s was probably taken so the family could share their grief with relatives in Italy who, for obvious reasons, could not attend the funeral in person.

VINCENT PERRY
BORN NOV 18-1900 DIED FEB 21-1917
DONATED BY PAURICI PASQUALE

F.HEIS

This elaborate funeral procession descended the Twenty-second Street hill from San Rocco. The close proximity of the Heller Chemical building on the left and the residential row on the right illustrates the mixed-use nature of the Hill neighborhood.

Ten

SCHOOLS

Public and private schools have been the pride of Chicago Heights, as well as a symbol of the community's progressiveness. Washington School, Old Bloom, and "new" Bloom provided for the diverse population a common experience and a common opportunity that created upward social mobility for all.

School kids posed in front of the original Washington School on Chicago Road in this *c.* 1900 photo taken before Fifteenth Street was extended west beyond Chicago Road.

Alma Mater. The stately appearance of Bloom Township High School in the 1920s makes it obvious why this institution was the pride of Chicago Heights. Built in 1901, the building closed in 1934. After the Halsted Street City Hall burned down in 1953, this building was used as the City Hall, Police/Fire Station, a roller rink, and a youth center called "The Morgue."

Bloom football players practiced on the grounds of Old Bloom c. 1920. Note the Fifteenth Street home in the background. It's still there.

On February 6, 1934, students moved their desks and other equipment to the new Bloom High School. In 1982, this handsome art deco structure was included in the National Register of Historic Places as a national landmark.

Three Bloom teachers, Myra Parkinson (Home Economics), Constance Mitchell (Latin), and Frances Russell (Commercial), from left to right, strolled along the campus walk in winter c. 1915.

Graduating McKinley School eighth graders had a mixture of smiles and pensive looks for the camera in this 1923 photo.

Boys of the Lincoln School posed for this photo in 1935.

Eleven

INDUSTRY

By the 1920s, there were only a few products, from rails to shoe strings, that were <u>not</u> manufactured in Chicago Heights. Plentiful industrial jobs for city residents were the basis for the city's prosperity and growth, as well as the success of ethnic newcomers and their families. It is difficult for the modern observer to understand the amount of sacrifice given by industrial workers in the first half of the century. Environmental concerns were low on the list of the town's leaders and citizens. Besides, the factories were on the east end of the city and the prevailing winds were from the west.

Steel workers posed for a lunchtime photo *c.* 1929.

Standard Lumber Yard, located on East Main Street in the 1920s, provided building materials for an expanding region. Note the three-digit phone numbers, clay drainage tiles, conveyor belts, and the proximity of the yard to the Giant factory.

The Hicks Locomotive Works Coach Department employees showed diversity in work apparel c. 1920. Hicks was a major East Side employer.

The Bonnet-Nance Stove Company, located at Seventeenth and Wentworth, gave employment to scores of workers. Above, workers posed with the molded metal parts of the fancy wood and coal-burning stoves of the day c. 1920.

A photo of the executive office of stove manufacturer J.J. Bonnet (standing) reveals an all-male secretarial staff working with antique office machinery.

Employees at the terra-cotta works included skilled craftsmen who provided terra-cotta trim for buildings nationwide, especially in the Chicago area. The Flat Iron and the Chicago Heights National Bank buildings both used locally produced terra-cotta in their exterior decor.

One of the premier employers in Chicago Heights was Amsco. Until its demise in 1980, the manganese alloy company at Fourteenth and State Streets provided blue- and white-collar employment for thousands. Italian-American workers, especially, seemed to gravitate to Amsco. This white-collar group posed outside the plant in 1931.

Little Giant's 1-ton trucks were manufactured entirely in Chicago Heights from 1910 to the early 1920s. The plant, which was located on the East Side, was worth $2,000,000 in 1919. The number employed at the plant in 1913 was reported at 75.

The Hildeman Plumbing employees built this on-site tool shed in the early 1930s when they had the contract for the plumbing at the new Bloom Township High School.

Well-dressed strikers at a Chicago Heights plant in the 1930s included several African Americans, as well as women and children. This peaceful conflict appears to be typical of Chicago Heights. Despite the fact that the city included large steel, chemical, and roofing plants, evidence of violent labor disputes is minimal.

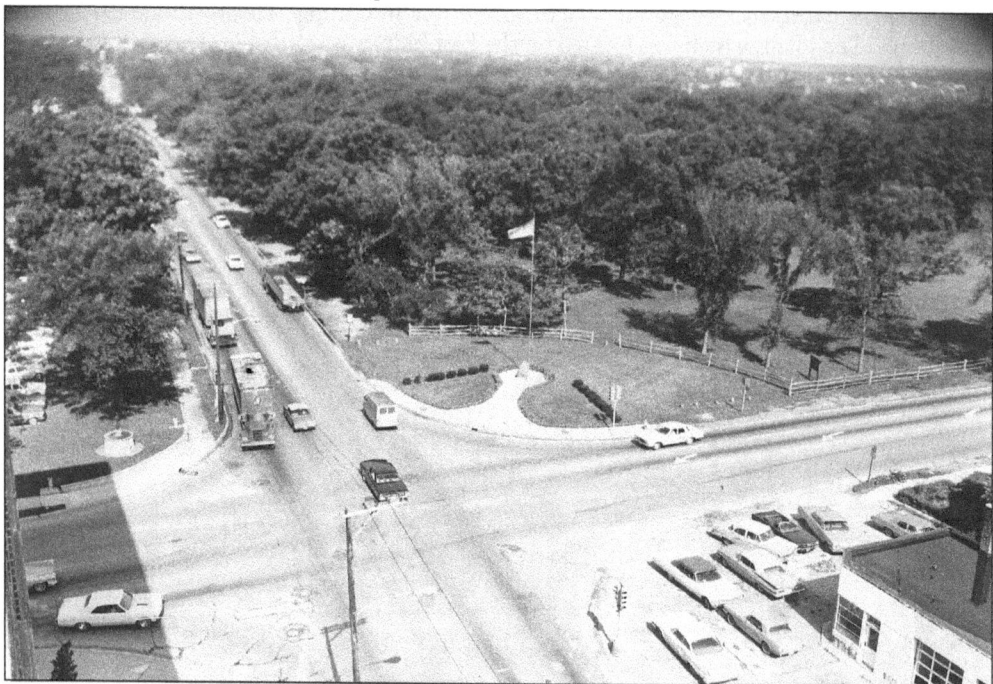

This view from the 1960s shows the Lincoln-Dixie Crossroads of the Nation looking west from St. James Hospital, with Woodrow Wilson Woods and the West Side in the background. The Chicago Heights Builders Club later constructed a plaza around the rock military monument.

128

Visit us at
arcadiapublishing.com